DATE DUE

PRINTED IN U.S.A.

Homes in the Wild

Homes in the Wild

Where Baby Animals and Their Parents Live

Lita Judge

ROARING BROOK PRESS
New York

Every animal needs a home.

A home might be as simple as a tree. This **brown-throated three-toed sloth** baby clings to his mother while she climbs branches like you do a jungle gym. Here, they find leaves to eat and safety from predators. Mother and baby feel so safe in the trees that they come down to the ground only about once a week to pee and poop.

Baby **European rabbits** are born snug underground inside a
burrow. Their home is part of a walled-in city with an interconnected
network of tunnels and chambers, called a warren. Large
warrens can house hundreds of rabbits, and some
include over two thousand entrances for a
quick escape from foxes.

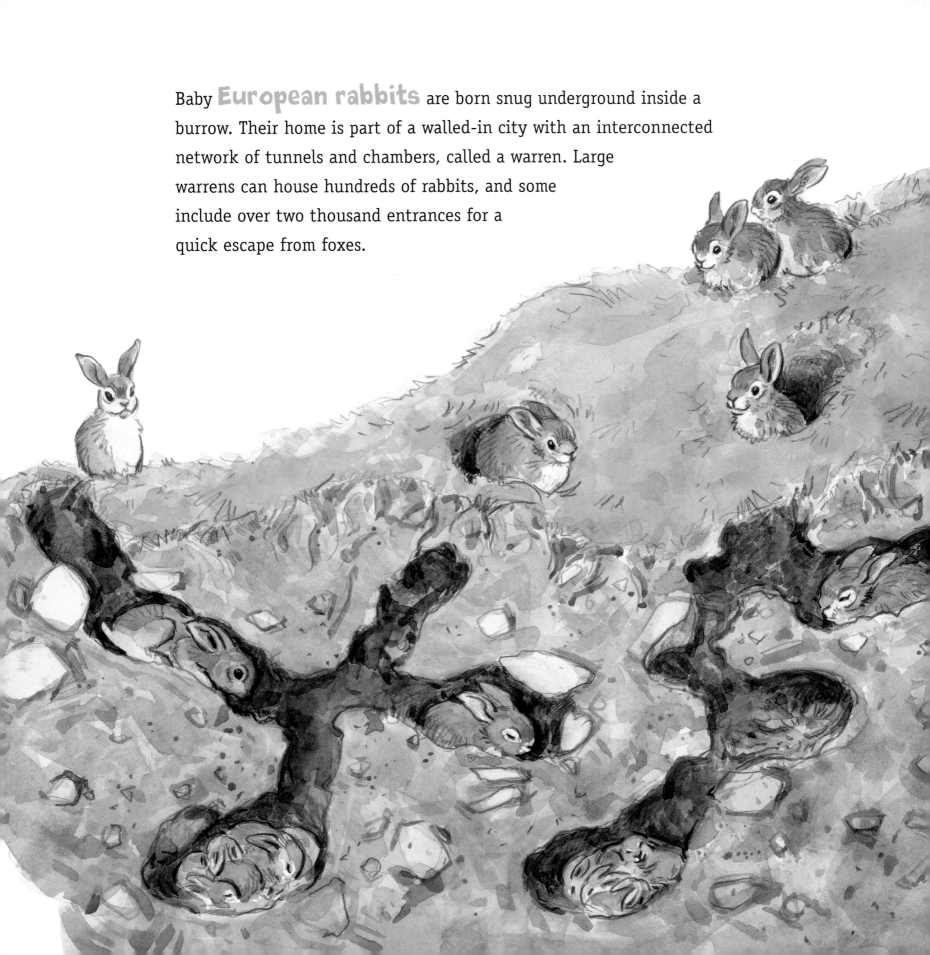

A home can be hidden.

Three **black bear** cubs peek out from their den under the roots of a tree. Their mother dug it the previous fall to hibernate in through winter. She also raked in leaves to make a comfy bed, where she gave birth to her cubs. Now it is spring, and soon her cubs will join her outside.

A **bobcat** litter stays safely hidden in a
rocky crevice that their mother has lined
with moss and grass. She leaves them for
long periods to hunt. When the cubs
are old enough, they will establish
their own territories and find
shelter within hollow logs,
under rocky ledges, or
in thickets of brush.

A baby **porcupine** stays hidden within a hollow
log in the daytime while his mother sleeps in a nearby
tree. She wakes up at night to forage for food and
nurse her baby. When he is old enough to
climb, he will sleep in his own tree.

A home can be

high in the trees.

A young **koala**, called a joey, clings to his mother's back while she climbs the limbs of a eucalyptus tree, which provides both a home and food. But eucalyptus leaves contain little nutrition, so the mother and joey conserve their energy by sleeping for about twenty hours a day.

High in the trees, golden snub-nosed monkeys find lichens, leaves, and bark to eat, and protection from predators like wolves and tigers. Their long limbs and tails make jumping from tree to tree and swinging on swaying branches look easy. At night they squeeze together with the babies in the center of the tree to keep them warm.

A baby silky anteater sleeps in a nest inside a tree hole. During the day, he rides on his father's back while his parents forage for ants. The family has golden fur that looks like the soft fiber seedpods of the silk-cotton kapok trees they live in. This camouflage makes it hard for predators to see them.

A home can be underground.

Coyote parents rarely dig a shelter to raise their pups in. They prefer to find a rocky crevice or an abandoned badger or fox den. Their pups stay safely hidden in their simple one-chamber den until they are about three to four weeks old, when they begin to venture out. Eventually, they will follow their parents to learn to hunt and patrol their territory.

A mother **long-eared jerboa** uses her mouse-sized paws and teeth to dig a complex burrow with several tunnels and entrances. Her home has food larders, sleeping chambers, and a nursery lined with grasses and camel hair where she raises her young. She even protects the burrow's entrances by making doors out of soil plugs to keep her burrow hidden and cool when the outside desert temperature soars to a furnace-like 120°F.

Baby **nine-banded armadillos** are also born in a world of cool darkness far belowground, safe from the desert sun and predators. Once they're grown, they will use their large, shovel-like claws to dig their own burrows. But one home isn't enough for an armadillo. As if building several weekend cottages, each one may dig up to twelve burrows scattered throughout its range.

A home can cover many miles of open country.

Animals with legs suited for walking or running rather than digging live in open rangeland. **Siberian tiger** cubs are born in a natal den, but within six months they join their mother in roaming a territory that can stretch up to four thousand square miles. Mother marks her territory with urine and scat and by rubbing against trees to leave behind her scent and hair. This tells other tigers it is her home. To make sure they get the message, she also scratches long slash marks on trees and in the ground.

A bonded pair of **dik-dik antelopes** works constantly to mark the boundaries of their home range. Together, they deposit urine and dung piles and rub their scent on twigs and blades of grass. Their fawn will stay safely hidden until she is old enough to roam with her parents. The family establishes a maze of trails, called runways, through the thick brush that they use to escape predators.

Mule deer and their fawns share their home range, migrating to different locations depending on the season. In summer they roam at higher elevations, but in winter they gather in herds in lower areas, where it isn't as snowy and cold. It may seem like they wander randomly, but in truth they keep to well-worn trails. At night and during the heat of the day, they bed down in a secluded place. You can find deer beds by looking for dung piles near oval areas of flattened grass.

A home can be
a cozy nest.

A woodpecker's old nest
makes a perfect winter
den for an **eastern gray
squirrel**. But in summer a
den can be hot, so many squirrels
build a home with natural air conditioning
by weaving dried leaves and twigs into a round
nest called a drey. Males build their own nests, while
females and their young share a nest. You can spot dreys
in winter, when the trees are bare, by looking for round
balls of leaves high up in the branches.

A **bushy-tailed woodrat** (or pack rat) builds a smaller nest inside a large stick den in a cave or rock crevasse. She might use cactus joints, pinecones, pieces of bone, and even cardboard and plastic for her building materials. These rats are attracted to shiny objects, like pieces of glass, foil, and coins. In fact, the name "pack rat" comes from their habit of collecting clutter. One small woodrat may build a den nine feet wide. Hold tight to your stuff if you camp near a pack rat's den!

An **eastern cottontail** doe (a female) makes a nest in a ground hollow or under a log when she is about to give birth. She lines her nest with grass or leaves. Finally, she plucks downy fur from her underside to warm her babies, who are born naked and helpless. Mother leaves the kittens when she goes to forage, but she visits her nest every night to nurse them. She pulls the soft, furry lining over them like a blanket before she leaves.

A home can be built
by an architect.

A mother **mountain gorilla** weaves a bed for herself and her baby out of branches and leaves. Every evening, as if practicing a bedtime ritual, she creates a new one even if the one they slept in the night before is just a few feet away. To build a ground nest, she bends branches into the center, then adds more plants, layering and anchoring them to one another. Sometimes, gorillas make their beds in trees instead.

A baby **orangutan** also sleeps in a bed his mother builds in a tree. Every day Mother pulls branches together, then braids them with smaller branches and leaves to make a mattress. She may even weave leaf pillows, blankets, and a rain roof. As her baby grows, she sometimes fashions a bunk bed for the two of them. At six months, he begins to practice building his own nest, but it will be nearly three years before he can make one by himself.

Perhaps the best animal architects are beavers. An entire family works together to fell small trees, using their teeth as saws. They swim the timber to the construction site and place it in an interlocking pattern to construct a lodge. Around that they build a dam, creating a moat-like pond to keep out predators. They dredge mud and stones from the bottom of the pond to seal the dam. Once the lodge is finished, the beavers chew tunnels through the walls to create underwater entrances that make it a safe haven for the year's litter of one to four kits.

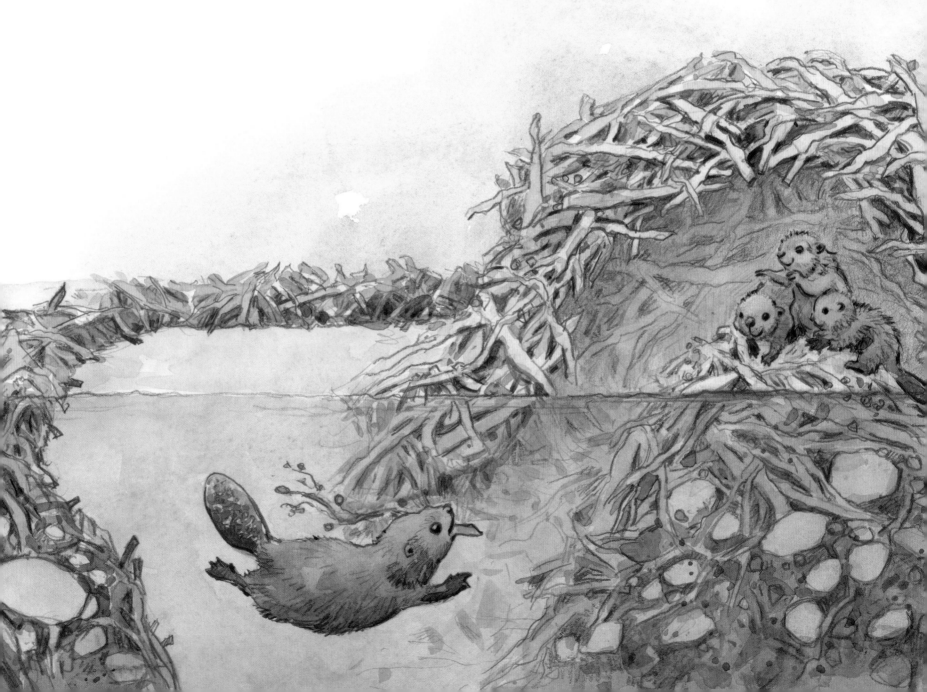

A home can

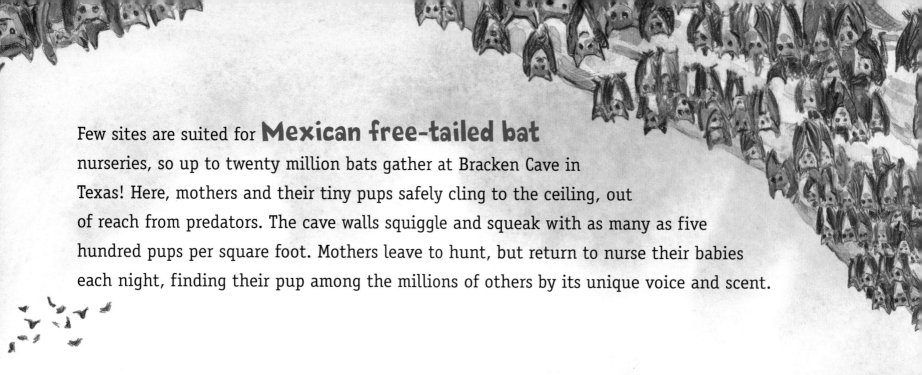

Few sites are suited for **Mexican free-tailed bat** nurseries, so up to twenty million bats gather at Bracken Cave in Texas! Here, mothers and their tiny pups safely cling to the ceiling, out of reach from predators. The cave walls squiggle and squeak with as many as five hundred pups per square foot. Mothers leave to hunt, but return to nurse their babies each night, finding their pup among the millions of others by its unique voice and scent.

Each family of **black-tailed prairie dogs**, called a coterie, finds safety by living close to other family groups. Together, they make a neighborhood, or ward. Several wards make up a town that can span hundreds of acres. The members of this close-knit community defend the invisible boundaries of their homes by forming a neighborhood alert system. If danger comes near, they warn one another by barking loudly.

California sea lions make their homes mostly in the sea, but move ashore to mate and raise young. Many mothers return to the same beaches where their mothers and grandmothers raised their pups. Like overcrowded preschools, some colonies, called rookeries, are inhabited by ten thousand sea lions. While the pups nurse, rest, and grow, their mothers protect them from harm.

be crowded.

A home can be borrowed.

Many animals don't build their own homes.
A mother **river otter** finds a perfect
home, called a holt or couch, in a beaver lodge.
Occasionally she and her pups share the lodge
with the beavers, but usually she finds one
that's been abandoned. The dammed pond
around the lodge is brimming with fish and
crayfish to feed her family, and the lodge's
underwater entrances keep the family safe from
predators. Mother even makes a comfy nest
inside the den by adding fresh moss and leaves.

Northern flying squirrels sometimes benefit from the hard work of woodpeckers. After these birds have drilled multiple holes in a dead tree, the cavities become an apartment complex for other species of birds and animals. A colony of squirrels, which includes parents, their young, and the year's babies, occupies one cavity as a natal nest.

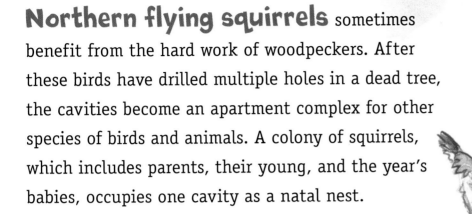

Raccoons den in fallen logs and tree cavities. But as sprawling human towns shrink their natural habitat, raccoons have adjusted to urban living. A mother and her kits in need of a warm, dry shelter may claim a barn, crawl space under a house, or attic as their own. With their dexterous fingers and clever minds, they easily adapt to new food sources too, raiding trash cans, bird feeders, and dog food bowls.

Pups, kits, cubs, and joeys—all baby animals need a home where they and their families are safe and sheltered . . .

just like you!

More about the animals in this book

Brown-throated three-toed sloths are lethargic because the tough, rubbery rain forest leaves they eat provide little nutrition. Their limbs are so well adapted for life in the trees that they can barely walk on the ground. They are about the size of a house cat. Algae can grow in their thick brown fur, leaving a green tint that serves as camouflage. They are found in the tropical rain forests of South and Central America. Females give birth to a single baby each year.

European rabbits live in colonies composed of many families. Mother rabbits create soft nests of fur in nursery chambers for their babies, who are born blind, furless, and helpless. Multiple warren entrances ensure that there is always a door nearby to escape through if a predator comes too close. Although they're native to southwestern Europe, these rabbits now live all around the world. A female can have several litters of five or six babies a year.

American black bears are native to North America. Bears enter their dens in late fall to hibernate through the winter. As they hibernate, their hearts beat only about eight times a minute rather than the usual forty to fifty, but their body temperature does not drop significantly, unlike in other hibernating animals. If the winter is mild, adult bears may rouse themselves and go foraging for food. Females give birth in January or February, usually to two or three cubs.

Bobcats range throughout most of North America. Males and females come together to mate, but otherwise, these mostly nocturnal animals keep to themselves in territories they mark with their scent. Bobcats are excellent hunters, crouching for long periods to watch and listen, then pouncing quickly to take down prey. Females can give birth to litters of one to six kittens, but usually there are two or three. The kittens begin learning to hunt when they are five months old.

North American porcupines are slow, mainly nocturnal rodents. Their coat of about thirty thousand quills covers their back, sides, and tail. Quills are modified hairs that are sharp, barbed, and hollow—perfect for defense. Because porcupines often fall out of trees as they're foraging, their skin has antibiotics that prevent infection when they are stuck by their own quills. Babies, called porcupettes, are born with soft quills that soon harden. One baby is born to each female.

Koalas are slow animals inhabiting the eucalyptus woodlands of southern and eastern Australia. They are marsupials, giving birth to a single embryonic joey weighing less than 0.02 ounces. Naked and blind, the joey crawls up and into his mother's pouch immediately after birth, where he develops and grows for six to seven months. He is completely weaned and independent by twelve months of age.

Golden snub-nosed monkeys live in the mountain forests of central and southwestern China. They live in groups of one male and up to ten females and their young. The females in a group care for one another's babies and groom each other. When a predator comes near, the male sounds the alarm while the females cling together in tightly packed groups with their babies in the center. Females give birth to one infant each year.

Silky anteaters (or pygmy anteaters) are the smallest of all anteaters and live in the lowland rain forests of Central and South America. They are nocturnal and arboreal, living where continuous tree canopy lets them travel without climbing down to the ground. A female gives birth to a single baby once or twice a year. Both parents raise their baby, feeding it regurgitated (spit-up) insects. An adult silky anteater can eat up to five thousand ants a day.

Coyotes are found throughout much of North and Central America. Some live alone or in pairs, but others live in family groups called packs. Pack members often travel and hunt alone, but use long howls to communicate. Coyote pups are dependent on their mother's milk for about a month and then begin eating solid food regurgitated by their parents. At around six weeks, the pups are given rodents, rabbits, birds, or pieces of larger carcasses.

A **long-eared jerboa** is a nocturnal rodent that can jump ten feet long or seven feet high and hop at sixteen miles per hour to escape. To cope with the frigid winters in Mongolia's Gobi Desert, the jerboas that live there hibernate. Jerboas that live in the hot Sahara Desert wait out the blistering summers in a light hibernation state called torpor. Females give birth two or three times a year to litters of two to six (usually three) pups.

Nine-banded armadillos give birth to four young who are always identical quadruplets. Armadillos have sensitive noses that can detect insects eight inches underground. Their strange appearance comes from their armored carapace, a bony case covered with tough skin that protects them from predators. Nine-banded armadillos live in forests, grasslands, and scrublands in Central and South America and in southern North America.

Siberian tigers are the largest cat species, reaching up to eleven feet long and weighing as much as seven hundred pounds. They are endangered in the wild, with only about five hundred remaining in pockets of southeastern Russia, along with a few in northeastern China and perhaps in North Korea. A mother tiger gives birth to a litter of one to six cubs. They are weaned at five to six months. Cubs stay with their mother for two to three years.

Kirk's dik-diks are small antelopes. They stand just fourteen to eighteen inches high at the shoulders and weigh seven to sixteen pounds. Common in the arid, dry scrublands of eastern Africa, they rarely have access to water. They get the moisture they need from the morning dew and their diet of primarily leaves and grass. Dik-diks are named for their alarm calls, which are made by whistling through their noses.

Mule deer range throughout much of western North America. Unlike the females (does), the males (bucks or stags) have antlers that grow in the spring and are shed each winter. Mule deer mate in November and December. During those months, called the rut, bucks fight one another for the chance to breed. In the summer, the does go off alone to give birth, usually to two fawns. Fawns have a reddish coat with white spots, which helps them hide in the brush. These spots fade within a few months.

Eastern gray squirrels are rodents native to eastern North America. Females bear litters of one to eight young twice a year. Gray squirrels prefer mature forests of oak, walnut, beech, and hickory trees because their nuts can be used for food year-round. During winter, these squirrels don't hibernate and need the snug tree dens they build to protect them from the cold.

Bushy-tailed woodrats (or pack rats) are cliff-dwellers who occupy higher-elevation woodlands and deserts in western North America. Females have up to three litters of one to six offspring each year. Nests are usually located within a pile called a midden that is both a bathroom and a garbage dump. Multiple generations of pack rats may contribute to the same midden. Some reach ten feet high and ten feet wide!

The **eastern cottontail** is common in the eastern half of the United States, much of Mexico, and northern South America. Before mating, a male (buck) and female (doe) do a mating dance in which the buck chases the doe until she turns around to face him and boxes at him with her front paws. Then one of them jumps straight up in the air and the other does the same. Does can have one to seven litters each year, each with an average of five babies.

Mountain gorillas are critically endangered due to loss of habitat and illegal hunting. Only two wild populations remain, both in dense mountain rain forests in central Africa. Family groups are very close-knit and usually consist of one older male called a silverback (for the silvery gray hairs on his back), three females, and four or five of their young. Females will have only one baby every four to five years. Newborn gorillas are weak and tiny, weighing only about four pounds.

Orangutans, found in the rain forests of Sumatra and Borneo, are endangered. They are the only great ape that lives primarily in trees. Only humans have a longer-lasting relationship with their young than a mother orangutan does with her single offspring. She will nurse him until he is about six years old. Baby orangutans mature slowly, and young males stay with their mothers until they are eight to ten years old, while females may remain into their teens.

North American beavers are large rodents that eat primarily leaves and the sugary inner bark of trees. Male and female beavers mate for life. A beaver has four front teeth enriched with iron, making them extra hard for felling trees. Those teeth never stop growing, so they won't wear down from all the gnawing. The beaver's broad, stiff tail works like a boat's rudder, helping the animal steer through the water, and it can be slapped loudly on the water's surface to warn others when danger is near.

California sea lions are native to the western coast of North America. They dive up to twelve hundred feet deep in search of fish and squid to eat. They can also swim about eighteen miles per hour for short bursts when escaping from killer whales and sharks. The females give birth to a single pup. Pups are born with dense fur to keep them warm until they can develop a layer of blubber from their mother's rich milk.

Mexican free-tailed bats, also called Brazilian free-tailed bats, are native to much of North and South America. The beating wings of a flock of twenty million sounds like the roaring of a white-water river. Bats use echolocation (producing sound waves that bounce off objects and are reflected back to the bat) to locate food (flying insects) and avoid obstacles. Individuals can recognize their own pulse reflections, or "voice." Each year, mothers give birth to one pup.

Black-tailed prairie dogs are rodents native to the Great Plains of North America. Family coteries consist of a dominant male and several females raising their young cooperatively. Females give birth to a litter of usually three pups and remain in the group they were born in for life. Males leave these groups once they are grown. Coterie members maintain strong bonds by touching their front teeth together, called "kissing," and by sniffing and grooming one another.

North American river otters are semi-aquatic. Males and females interact only during the mating season, but a mother and her young pups form a family group called a bevy or romp. Females give birth to one to six pups that stay in their den for eight to ten weeks before learning how to swim and hunt. River otters have webbed feet, and their nostrils and ears close underwater. They are known for their playfulness.

Northern flying squirrels are found in forests in North America. You may never see these nocturnal animals. Sometimes they shift from nest to nest after raising their young. They may store seeds and nuts for winter food in extra boxes or dens. Flying squirrels can't fly like birds. Instead, they glide up to 150 feet by stretching out a skin membrane that connects each front paw to the back paw on the same side.

Raccoons are common throughout most of North America. Unlike most wild animals, raccoons' intelligence and dexterous front paws have allowed them to adapt to living among people as human settlements have shrunk their natural habitats. In suburbia and cities, raccoons use their deft fingers to open trash cans, even when they have to first open a garage or shed door to access them. Females have one to seven kits in the early summer.

Glossary

arboreal—An animal who lives in the trees

dung—The poop of a plant-eating animal

forage—To search for food

habitat—The natural home or environment of an animal

larder—A place for storing food

nurse—To feed a baby animal milk from the mother's breast

predator—An animal that kills and eats other animals (the prey)

prey—An animal that is killed and eaten by another animal (the predator)

scat—An animal's feces

Sources

Elbroch, Mark, and Kurt Rinehart. *Peterson Reference Guide to the Behavior of North American Mammals*. Boston: Houghton Mifflin Harcourt, 2011.

Estes, Richard. *The Behavior Guide to African Mammals: Including Hoofed Mammals, Carnivores, Primates*. Illustrated by Daniel Otte. Berkeley, CA: University of California Press, 2012.

Gardner, Alfred L., ed. *Mammals of South America*. Vol. 1. Chicago: University of Chicago Press, 2007.

Macdonald, David W., ed. *The Princeton Encyclopedia of Mammals*. Princeton, NJ: Princeton University Press, 2009.

Menkhorst, Peter, and Frank Knight. *A Field Guide to the Mammals of Australia*. New York: Oxford University Press, 2011.

National Geographic Society. *National Geographic Book of Mammals*. Washington, DC: National Geographic, 1998.

Nowak, Ronald M. *Walker's Mammals of the World*. Baltimore, MD: Johns Hopkins University Press, 1999.

Parker, Steve. *DK Eyewitness Books: Mammal*. New York: DK, 2004.

Reid, Fiona A. *A Field Guide to Mammals of North America, North of Mexico*. Boston: Houghton Mifflin, 2006.

Good Websites for More Information on Animal Homes

Animal Diversity Web: animaldiversity.org

BBC Nature: bbc.co.uk/nature/wildlife

Enchanted Learning: enchantedlearning.com/subjects/animals/Animalbabies.shtml

Encyclopedia of Life: eol.org

National Geographic: animals.nationalgeographic.com/animals

National Wildlife Federation: nwf.org/Wildlife.aspx

Ranger Rick: rangerrick.org

World Animal Foundation: worldanimal.foundation

For Dave, who shares my home in the woods

Library of Congress Control Number: 2018039601
ISBN: 978-1-62672-724-3

Our books may be purchased in bulk for promotional, educational, or business use. Please contact your local
bookseller or the Macmillan Corporate and Premium Sales Department at (800) 221-7945 ext. 5442 or by email
at MacmillanSpecialMarkets@macmillan.com.

First edition, 2019
Book design by Monique Sterling
Printed in China by RR Donnelley Asia Printing Solutions Ltd., Dongguan City, Guangdong Province

1   3   5   7   9   10   8   6   4   2